This journal belongs to

....

My Heart's Prayer

a prayer journal

© 2009 Ellie Claire Gift & Paper Corp.

www.ellieclaire.com

Compiled by Joanie Garborg

Designed by Lisa & Jeff Franke

Special thanks to Marilyn Jansen for the use of her original prayers. For the last thirteen years
Marilyn has worked as a writer and editor of inspirational gift products.

Scripture references are from the following sources: The Holy Bible, King James Version (KJV): The New King James
Version (NKJV). Copyright © 1982 by Thomas Nelson, Inc. Used by permission. The Holy Bible, English Standard Version®
(ESV), copyright © 2001 by Crossway Bibles, a publishing ministry of Good News Publishers. Used by permission.
The New American Standard Bible® (NASB), Copyright © 1960, 1962, 1963, 1968, 1971, 1972, 1973, 1975, 1977,
1995 by The Lockman Foundation. Used by permission. The Holy Bible, New International Version®, NIV®
Copyright © 1973, 1978, 1984 by International Bible Society. Used by permission of Zondervan. The Holy Bible,
New Living Translation (NLT), copyright 1996, 2004. Used by permission of Tyndale House Publishers, Inc., Wheaton,
Illinois. *The Message.* Copyright © 1993, 1994, 1995, 1996, 2000, 2001, 2002. Used by permission of NavPress,
Colorado Springs, CO. All rights reserved.

In some quotations, pronouns such as *thee* and *thy* have been changed to *you* and *your* and verbs such
as *cometh* and *shalt* have been changed to more modern forms.

ISBN 978-1-935416-10-4

Printed in China

*G*reat is the Lord, and greatly to be praised;
And His greatness is unsearchable.
One generation shall praise Your works to another,
And shall declare Your mighty acts.

PSALM 145:3-4 NKJV

The Lord's Prayer is a floor plan of the house of God: a step-by-step description of how God meets our needs when we dwell in Him. Everything that occurs in a healthy house is described in this prayer. Protection, instruction, forgiveness, provision...all occur under God's roof.

MAX LUCADO

The Lord's Prayer

Our Father which art in heaven,
Hallowed be thy name.
Thy kingdom come.
Thy will be done in earth,
as it is in heaven.
Give us this day our daily bread.
And forgive us our debts,
as we forgive our debtors.
And lead us not into temptation,
but deliver us from evil:
For thine is the kingdom, and the power,
and the glory, for ever.
Amen.

Matthew 6:9-13 KJV

Prayers Not Prayed

If there are any tears shed in heaven, they will be over the fact that we prayed so little.
Heaven is full of answers to prayer for which no one ever bothered to ask.

BILLY GRAHAM

Prayer Requests

Answers to Prayer

*K*eep on asking, and you will receive what you ask for. Keep on seeking, and you will find. Keep on knocking, and the door will be opened to you. For everyone who asks, receives. Everyone who seeks, finds. And to everyone who knocks, the door will be opened.

MATTHEW 7:7-8 NLT

A Prayer of Adoration

Lord Jesus Christ, You are the sun that always rises, but never sets. You are the source of all life, creating and sustaining every living thing. You are the source of all food, material and spiritual, nourishing us in both body and soul. You are the light that dispels the clouds of error and doubt. May I walk to Your light, be nourished by Your food, be sustained by Your mercy, and be warmed by Your love.

ERASMUS

Prayer Requests

Answers to Prayer

The LORD is my light and my salvation; whom shall I fear?
The LORD is the strength of my life; of whom shall I be afraid?

PSALM 27:1 NKJV

A Prayer of Gratitude for Family

Heavenly Father,
Thank You for my wonderful family. Even though we are not perfect, I praise You for this group of people that You have ordained as those who will be closest to me. Help me to be the best wife, mother, and woman that I can be—today and every day of my life. Amen.

KIM BOYCE

Prayer Requests

Answers to Prayer

*G*OD's love...is ever and always, eternally present to all who fear him,
making everything right for them and their children as they follow
his Covenant ways and remember to do whatever he said.

PSALM 103:17-18 THE MESSAGE

Hallowed Be Thy Name...

Lord, I praise You. I magnify Your name. I am daily amazed by Your grace and mercy. You are the heart of my life. Without You my life is incomplete. With You I have everything I need. I worship and praise Your name. Amen.

MARILYN JANSEN

Prayer Requests

Answers to Prayer

O Lᴏʀᴅ, our Lord, how majestic is your name in all the earth!
You have set your glory above the heavens.

Pꜱᴀʟᴍ 8:1 ᴇꜱᴠ

Reasons to Pray

People sometimes say that the only reason for prayer is that we need to be changed.
Certainly we do, but that is not the only reason to pray. Jesus was not being made
more holy by prayer. He was communing with His Father. He was asking for things.
He thanked God. He was also laying down His own will.

ELISABETH ELLIOT

Prayer Requests

Answers to Prayer

Reflections and Praise

$\mathscr{T}$he earnest prayer of a righteous person has great power
and produces wonderful results.

JAMES 5:16 NLT

A Prayer of Wonder

Dear Lord, grant me the grace of wonder. Surprise me, amaze me, awe me in every
crevice of Your universe. Delight me to see how Your Christ plays in ten thousand
places...to the Father through the features of men's faces. Each day enrapture me
with Your marvelous things without number. I do not ask to see the reason for it all;
I ask only to share the wonder of it all.

ABRAHAM JOSHUA HESCHEL

Prayer Requests

Answers to Prayer

You answer us with awesome deeds of righteousness, O God our Savior,
the hope of all the ends of the earth and of the farthest seas....
Where morning dawns and evening fades You call forth songs of joy.

PSALM 65:5, 8 NIV

A Prayer for Rest

Slow me down, Lord....
Remind me each day
That the race is not always won by the fastest runner;
That there is more to life than increasing its speed.

WILFERD A. PETERSON

Prayer Requests

Answers to Prayer

*L*et the beloved of the LORD rest secure in him, for he shields him all day long,
and the one the LORD loves rests between his shoulders.

DEUTERONOMY 33:12 NIV

Worship God in His glory. Think of what He can do, and how He delights to hear the prayers of His redeemed people. Think of your place and privilege in Christ, and expect great things!

ANDREW MURRAY

A Prayer of Worship

How lovely is your dwelling place,
O Lord of hosts!
My soul longs, yes, faints
for the courts of the Lord;
my heart and flesh sing for joy
to the living God....
Blessed are those who dwell in your house,
ever singing your praise!
Blessed are those whose strength is in you,
in whose heart are the highways to Zion....
They go from strength to strength;
each one appears before God in Zion....
For a day in your courts is better
than a thousand elsewhere....
The Lord God is a sun and shield;
the Lord bestows favor and honor.
No good thing does he withhold
from those who walk uprightly.
O Lord of hosts,
blessed is the one who trusts in you!

PSALM 84:1-2, 4-5, 7, 10-12 ESV

God Is in Control

Heavenly Father, there are times when I feel so overwhelmed and out of control with life. I don't know what to do and I begin to panic. Please bring Your love and peace to my spirit and help me to remember that it is You who is in control of everything in my life and in this world. Amen.

MARILYN JANSEN

Prayer Requests

Answers to Prayer

Reflections and Praise

*C*ome, behold the works of the LORD....
Be still, and know that I am God.

PSALM 46:8, 10 ESV

A Prayer for Forgiveness

Forgive us if this day we have done or said anything to increase the pain of the world.
Pardon the unkind word, the impatient gesture, the hard and selfish deed,
the failure to show sympathy and kindly help where we had the opportunity,
but missed it; and enable us so to live that we may daily do something to lessen
the tide of human sorrow and add to the sum of human happiness.

F. B. MEYER

Prayer Requests

....
....
....
....
....
....
....
....

Answers to Prayer

....
....
....
....
....
....
....
....

Reflections and Praise

*Be kind to one another, tenderhearted, forgiving one another,
as God in Christ forgave you.*

EPHESIANS 4:32 ESV

Prayer Changes Us

To pray is to change. This is a great grace. How good of God to provide a path
whereby our lives can be taken over by love and joy and peace and patience
and kindness and goodness and faithfulness and gentleness and self-control.

RICHARD J. FOSTER

Prayer Requests

Answers to Prayer

The acts of the sinful nature are obvious.... But the fruit of the Spirit is love, joy, peace, patience, kindness, goodness, faithfulness, gentleness and self-control.

GALATIANS 5:19, 22-23 NIV

Thy Kingdom Come...

Lord Jesus Christ
alive and at large in the world,
help me to follow and find You there today,
in the places where I work, meet people,
spend money, and make plans.

JOHN TAYLOR

Prayer Requests

Answers to Prayer

Reflections and Praise

*T*ake your everyday, ordinary life—your sleeping, eating, going-to-work, and walking-around life—and place it before God as an offering.... Don't become so well-adjusted to your culture that you fit into it without even thinking. Instead, fix your attention on God.

ROMANS 12:1-2 THE MESSAGE

Longing for God

We desire many things and [God] offers us only one thing. He can offer us only one thing—
Himself. He has nothing else to give. There is nothing else to give.

PETER KREEFT

Prayer Requests

Answers to Prayer

*W*hom have I in heaven but You? And besides You, I desire nothing on earth. My flesh
and my heart may fail, but God is the strength of my heart and my portion forever....
As for me, the nearness of God is my good; I have made the LORD God my refuge.

PSALM 73:25-26, 28 NASB

A Prayer to Be Used

Thank You, Father, for putting me right where I am. So many times I've heard,
"bloom where you are planted." Help me to do that. Help me take whatever gifts
and talents You have given me and use them to make the world a better place.
Help me to spread Your love from where I am right now. Amen.

MARILYN JANSEN

Prayer Requests

Answers to Prayer

Reflections and Praise

*S*ince we have gifts that differ according to the grace given to us,
each of us is to exercise them accordingly.

ROMANS 12:6 NASB

Lord, Help Me Pray

There are times when we may have to pray, "Lord, I don't feel like trusting; I don't feel like praying, but I want to want to." Whatever we have, even if it's only our questions and doubts and uncertainties, if we will just abandon them to Him, He will take them.

GLORIA GAITHER

Prayer Requests

Answers to Prayer

O my people, trust in him at all times. Pour out your heart to him,
for God is our refuge.

PSALM 62:8 NLT

He will endure as long as the sun, as long as the moon, through all generations....
He will rule from sea to sea and from the River to the ends of the earth.

PSALM 72:5, 8 NIV

....

....

....

....

....

....

....

....

....

....

....

....

....

....

....

....

....

A Prayer of Trust

Dear Lord, today I thought of the words of
Vincent van Gogh, "It is true that there is an
ebb and flow, but the sea remains the sea."

You are the sea. Although I may experience many ups
and downs in my emotions and often feel great shifts
in my inner life, You remain the same. Your sameness
is not the sameness of a rock, but the sameness of a
faithful lover. Out of Your love I came to life; by Your
love I am sustained; and to Your love I am always
called back. There are days of sadness and days of joy;
there are feelings of guilt and feelings of gratitude;
there are moments of failure and moments of success;
but all of them are embraced by Your unwavering love.

My only real temptation is to doubt Your love, to think
of myself as beyond the reach of Your love, to remove
myself from the healing radiance of Your love. To do
these things is to move into the darkness of despair.

O Lord, sea of love and goodness, let me not fear
too much the storms and winds of my daily life,
and let me know that there is ebb and flow…
but that the sea remains the sea.
Amen.

HENRI J. M. NOUWEN

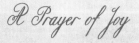

A Prayer of Joy

Heavenly Father,
Thank You for the opportunity to laugh. Help me to find joy in everything that I do.
Let me laugh and be cheerful, so that those around me will be blessed by my
smile and my optimism. Amen.

KIM BOYCE

Prayer Requests

Answers to Prayer

Reflections and Praise

*S*atisfy us in the morning with your unfailing love, that we may
sing for joy and be glad all our days.

PSALM 90:14 NIV

Times of Prayer

Ah! How often...has God kissed you at the beginning of prayer, and spoken peace to you in the midst of prayer, and filled you with joy and assurance upon the close of prayer!

THOMAS BROOKS

Prayer Requests

Answers to Prayer

*Evening and morning and at noon I will pray, and cry aloud,
and He shall hear my voice.*

PSALM 55:17 NKJV

Lord, Send Me

Dearest Jesus, help me to remember that, whether I want to be or not, I am Your
ambassador on earth. What the world experiences of Your love, sincerity, and holiness
is experienced through people like me. Help me to remember that when
I reach out to others, I am reaching in Your name. That when I share Your word,
they are hearing You. That when I do neither, they feel as if You passed them by.
Jesus, help me to be a good ambassador. Amen.

MARILYN JANSEN

Prayer Requests

....
....
....
....
....
....

Answers to Prayer

....
....
....
....
....
....
....
....

How can they believe in him if they have never heard about him? And how can
they hear about him unless someone tells them? And how will anyone go
and tell them without being sent?

ROMANS 10:14–15 NLT

Thy Will Be Done...

Into Your hands, O Lord, we commend ourselves this day. Let Your presence be with us to its close. Strengthen us to remember that in whatever good work we do we are serving You. Give us a diligent and watchful spirit, that we may seek in all things to know Your will, and knowing it, gladly to perform it, to the honor and glory of Your name; through Jesus Christ our Lord.

GELASIAN SACRAMENTARY

Prayer Requests

....

....

....

....

....

....

Answers to Prayer

....

....

....

....

....

....

I delight to do Your will, O my God;
Your Law is within my heart.

PSALM 40:8 NASB

Prayer Changes Things

Your prayers move God to change the world. You may not understand
the mystery of prayer. You don't need to. But this much is clear: Actions in heaven
begin when someone prays on earth. What an amazing thought!

MAX LUCADO

Prayer Requests

Answers to Prayer

Reflections and Praise

That's why I urge you to pray for absolutely everything, ranging from small to large. Include everything as you embrace this God-life, and you'll get God's everything.

MARK 11:24 THE MESSAGE

A Prayer of Praise

O wisdom without end, O mercy without limit,
O strength beyond resistance, O crown of all majesty,
The humblest You created sings Your praise.

MECHTILD OF MAGDEBURG

Prayer Requests

Answers to Prayer

*A*s your name deserves, O God, you will be praised to the ends of the earth.
Your strong right hand is filled with victory.

PSALM 48:10 NLT

A Prayer of Love

Dear God, did I tell You I love You today? I do. I love You for just being You.
I love You for loving me. I love You for saving me, for providing for me,
for protecting me, for forgiving me. You're awesome, God, marvelous and
wonderful. Help me to glorify You in all I do. Amen.

MARILYN JANSEN

Prayer Requests

Answers to Prayer

I love you, O LORD, my strength. The LORD is my rock and my fortress
and my deliverer, my God, my rock, in whom I take refuge.

PSALM 18:1-2 ESV

I pray that your love for each other will overflow more and more, and that you will keep on growing in your knowledge and understanding.

PHILIPPIANS 1:9 NLT

A Prayer of Commitment

Now, into the keeping of God I put
All doings of today
All disappointments,
hindrances,
forgotten things,
negligences.
All gladness and beauty,
love,
delight,
achievement.
All that people have done for me,
All that I have done for them,
my work and my prayers.
And I commit all the people whom I love
to His shepherding,
to His healing and restoring,
to His calling and making;
Through Jesus Christ our Lord.

MARGARET CROPPER

Right and Good Answers

Praying unlocks the doors of heaven and releases the power of God.
God's answers are always right and good and best. Whether prayer changes
our situation or not, one thing is certain: Prayer will change us!

BILLY GRAHAM

Prayer Requests

....

....

....

....

....

....

Answers to Prayer

....

....

....

....

....

....

....

*N*ow I know that the LORD saves His anointed;
He will answer him from His holy heaven
With the saving strength of His right hand.

PSALM 20:6 NASB

Glory to God

Shine forth in splendor, You who are calm weather,
And quiet resting place for faithful souls.
To see You is the end and the beginning,
You carry us, and You go before,
You are the journey, and the journey's end.

BOETHIUS

Prayer Requests

Answers to Prayer

*Y*ours, O Lord, is the greatness and the power and the glory and the majesty
and the splendor, for everything in heaven and earth is yours. Yours, O Lord,
is the kingdom; you are exalted as head over all.

1 Chronicles 29:11 NIV

Lord, Teach Me to Pray

Jesus opens the door and grants us access into the heavenlies. Even more:
He straightens out and cleanses our feeble, misguided intercessions and makes
them acceptable before a holy God. Even more still: His prayers sustain our
desires to pray, urging us on and giving us hope of being heard.

RICHARD J. FOSTER

Prayer Requests

Answers to Prayer

*W*e do not know what we ought to pray for, but the Spirit himself intercedes for us....
And he who searches our hearts knows the mind of the Spirit, because the
Spirit intercedes for the saints in accordance with God's will.

ROMANS 8:26-27 NIV

Give Us This Day...

You only are the Maker of all things near and far;
You paint the wayside flower, You light the evening star;
The wind and waves obey You, by You the birds are fed;
Much more to us, Your children, You give our daily bread.

MATTHIUS CLAUDIUS, ADAPTED

Prayer Requests

....
....
....
....
....
....
....

Answers to Prayer

....
....
....
....
....
....
....
....
....

My God shall supply all your need according to His riches in glory by Christ Jesus.

PHILIPPIANS 4:19 NKJV

He Is the Answer

Lord, I have so many questions and so few answers. Reveal to me Your will.
Show me Your path and give me the wisdom to follow it. Feed me Your word, Lord.
Educate me in Your ways. When the questions of life are confusing or overwhelming,
remind me to wait on You, the one who has all the answers. Amen.

MARILYN JANSEN

Prayer Requests

Answers to Prayer

Reflections and Praise

That [your] hearts may be encouraged...to reach all the riches of full assurance of
understanding and the knowledge of God's mystery, which is Christ, in whom are
hidden all the treasures of wisdom and knowledge.

COLOSSIANS 2:2-3 ESV

A Prayer of Invitation

Come, my Light, and illumine my darkness.
Come, my Life, and revive me from death....
Come, Flame of divine love, and burn up the thorns of my sins,
kindling my heart with the flame of Your love.
Come, my King, sit upon the throne of my heart and reign there.
For You alone are my King and my Lord.

DIMITRII OF ROSTOV

Prayer Requests

....

....

....

....

....

....

....

Answers to Prayer

....

....

....

....

....

....

....

....

Reflections and Praise

*S*end forth your light and your truth, let them guide me; let them bring me
to your holy mountain, to the place where you dwell.

PSALM 43:3-4 NIV

A Prayer for an Eternal Focus

Heavenly Father,
Please give me the ability to see things as You see them. Help me to understand the importance of eternal things, and remind me not to focus so much energy on temporal things. May I be diligent in my home, yet more faithful to nurture the most important part of my home…my family. Amen.

KIM BOYCE

Prayer Requests

Answers to Prayer

I focus on this one thing: Forgetting the past and looking forward to what lies ahead,
I press on to reach the end of the race and receive the heavenly prize for which God,
through Christ Jesus, is calling us.

PHILIPPIANS 3:13-14 NLT

Let my soul take refuge...beneath the shadow of Your wings:
let my heart, this sea of restless waves, find peace in You, O God.

AUGUSTINE

A Prayer for Protection

Those who dwell in the shelter of the Most High
will abide in the shadow of the Almighty.
They will say to the Lord, "My refuge and my fortress,
my God, in whom I trust."
For you will deliver us from the snare of the fowler
and from the deadly pestilence.
You will cover us with your pinions,
and under your wings we will find refuge....
For you will command your angels concerning us
to guard us in all our ways.
On their hands they will bear us up,
lest we strike our foot against a stone....
When we hold fast to you in love, you will deliver us;
You will protect us, because we know your name.
When we call to you, you will answer us;
You will be with us in trouble;
You will rescue us and honor us.
With long life you will satisfy us
and show us your salvation.

PSALM 91:1-4, 11-12, 14-16 PARAPHRASED

Every Need Supplied

What God gives in answer to our prayers will always be the thing we most
urgently need, and it will always be sufficient.

ELISABETH ELLIOT

Prayer Requests

Answers to Prayer

Your Father already knows your needs. Seek the Kingdom of God above all else,
and he will give you everything you need.

LUKE 12:30-31 NLT

For the Beauty of the Earth

Dearest Creator of all things, I praise Your name. I praise Your creativity in making such a wondrous world. Just thinking of how all things on earth come together in such glorious harmonies is amazing. I don't have the words to adequately tell You how truly spectacular Your creation is to me. You are worthy of all praise. Amen.

MARILYN JANSEN

Prayer Requests

Answers to Prayer

You are worthy, our Lord and God, to receive glory and honor and power, for you
created all things, and by your will they were created and have their being.

REVELATION 4:11 NIV

Wait for the Lord

So wait before the Lord. Wait in the stillness. And in that stillness, assurance will come to you. You will know that you are heard; you will know that your Lord ponders the voice of your humble desires; you will hear quiet words spoken to you yourself, perhaps to your grateful surprise and refreshment.

AMY CARMICHAEL

Prayer Requests

Answers to Prayer

*W*ait for the LORD; be strong and let your heart take courage;
Yes, wait for the LORD.

PSALM 27:14 NASB

Forgive Our Trespasses...

O God, Father of all, help us to forgive others as we would wish them to forgive us.
May we try to understand them as we in turn would like to be understood, in the hope
that forgiveness will not be in order. May we see with their eyes, think with their minds,
feel with their hearts. Then let us ask ourselves whether we should judge them,
or judge ourselves and accept them as children, like us, of one heavenly Father.

WILLIAM BARCLAY

Prayer Requests

Answers to Prayer

Clothe yourselves with compassion, kindness, humility, gentleness and patience. Bear with each other and forgive whatever grievances you may have against one another. Forgive as the Lord forgave you.

COLOSSIANS 3:12-13 NIV

A Prayer of Longing

Lord Jesus Christ; Let me seek You by desiring You,
and let me desire You by seeking You;
let me find You by loving You,
and love You in finding You.

ANSELM

Prayer Requests

Answers to Prayer

As the deer pants for streams of water, so my soul pants for you, O God.
My soul thirsts for God, for the living God.

PSALM 42:1-2 NIV

A Prayer for Others

Loving God, I hold in Your healing presence and peace those whose needs are not known
to me but who are known by You, and those for whom I have been asked to pray....
And I name in my heart all those who are close to me...
May they know the deep peace of Christ.

IONA ABBEY WORSHIP BOOK

Prayer Requests

Answers to Prayer

In everything, by prayer and petition, with thanksgiving, present your
requests to God. And the peace of God, which transcends all understanding,
will guard your hearts and your minds in Christ Jesus.

PHILIPPIANS 4:6-7 NIV

A Prayer for Grace

Give me grace today, O Lord. Help me to be merciful to those who need mercy.
Help me to be kind to those who need kindness. Help me to be gentle with those who
need gentleness. Help me to be generous with those who need generosity. Help me to
be forgiving to those who ask for forgiveness. Help me to be more like You. Amen.

MARILYN JANSEN

Prayer Requests

Answers to Prayer

Reflections and Praise

*F*or you know the grace of our Lord Jesus Christ, that though he was rich, yet for your sakes he became poor, so that you through his poverty might become rich.

2 CORINTHIANS 8:9 NIV

Every good and perfect gift is from above, coming down from the Father of the heavenly lights, who does not change like shifting shadows.

JAMES 1:17 NIV

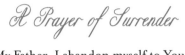

A Prayer of Surrender

My Father, I abandon myself to You.
Do with me as You will.
Whatever You may do with me, I thank You.
I am prepared for anything, I accept everything.
Provided Your will is fulfilled in me and in all
creatures, I ask for nothing more, my God.

I place my soul in Your hands.
I give it to You, my God,
with all the love of my heart
because I love You.
And for me it is a necessity of love,
this gift of myself,
this placing of myself in Your hands
without reserve
in boundless confidence
because You are my Father.

CHARLES DE FOUCAULD

A Response of Adoration

Prayer is the human response to the perpetual outpouring of love by which God lays siege to every soul. When our reply to God is most direct of all, it is called adoration. Adoration is spontaneous yearning of the heart to worship, honor, magnify, and bless God.

RICHARD J. FOSTER

Prayer Requests

....

....

....

....

....

....

....

Answers to Prayer

....

....

....

....

....

....

....

Reflections and Praise

*G*od is sheer being itself—Spirit. Those who worship him must do it out
of their very being, their spirits, their true selves, in adoration.

JOHN 4:24 THE MESSAGE

A Prayer for Change

Let the healing grace of Your love, O Lord, so transform me that I may play my part
in the transfiguration of the world from a place of suffering, death, and corruption
to a realm of infinite light, joy, and love. Make me so obedient to Your Spirit that
my life may become a living prayer, and a witness to Your unfailing presence.

MARTIN ISRAEL

Prayer Requests

Answers to Prayer

*N*othing between us and God, our faces shining with the brightness of his face.
And so we are transfigured...our lives gradually becoming brighter and more
beautiful as God enters our lives and we become like him.

2 CORINTHIANS 3:18 THE MESSAGE

The Lord Is with You

If the Lord is with us, we have no cause of fear. His eye is upon us, His arm over us,
His ear open to our prayer—His grace sufficient, His promise unchangeable.

JOHN NEWTON

Prayer Requests

....

....

....

....

....

....

....

....

Answers to Prayer

....

....

....

....

....

....

....

....

Be strong and courageous! Do not tremble or be dismayed,
for the LORD your God is with you wherever you go.

JOSHUA 1:9 NASB

Lead Us Not into Temptation...

Lord, protect me from temptation today. Strengthen me so I am able to say no!
Help me not to be blinded by my wants and desires or by my need to be like everybody else.
Help me to be different. Help me to stand firm, even if I stand by myself.
For I am never alone—You are always with me. Amen.

MARILYN JANSEN

Prayer Requests

Answers to Prayer

*N*o temptation has overtaken you but such as is common to man;
and God is faithful, who will not allow you to be tempted beyond what
you are able, but with the temptation will provide the way of escape.

1 CORINTHIANS 10:13 NASB

God Listens

You can talk to God because God listens. Your voice matters in heaven. He takes you very seriously. When you enter His presence, the attendants turn to you to hear your voice. No need to fear that you will be ignored. Even if you stammer or stumble, even if what you have to say impresses no one, it impresses God—and He listens.

MAX LUCADO

Prayer Requests

Answers to Prayer

If you make yourselves at home with me and my words are at home in you,
you can be sure that whatever you ask will be listened to and acted upon.

JOHN 15:7 THE MESSAGE

A Prayer of the Heart

Give me, Lord, a pure heart—that I may see You,
A humble heart—that I may hear You,
A heart of love—that I may serve You,
A heart of faith—that I may live You.

DAG HAMMARSKJÖLD

Prayer Requests

Answers to Prayer

You must love the LORD your God with all your heart,
all your soul, and all your mind.

MATTHEW 22:37 NLT

A Prayer to Choose Joy

Heavenly Father,

My prayer is that I would learn to trust You more. It's such a comfort to know that my life is in Your hands, and the circumstances surrounding me are in Your control. Remind me daily that choosing to be happy is an option. May I find my strength in Your joy. Amen.

KIM BOYCE

Prayer Requests

....
....
....
....
....
....
....

Answers to Prayer

....
....
....
....
....
....
....

Even though the fig trees have no blossoms, and there are no grapes
on the vines...yet I will rejoice in the LORD! I will be joyful in the
God of my salvation! The Sovereign LORD is my strength!

HABAKKUK 3:17-19 NLT

Be Thou my Vision, O Lord of my heart;
Naught be all else to me, save that Thou art.
Thou my best thought, by day or by night,
Waking or sleeping, Thy presence my light.

A Prayer of Comfort

O Lord, you have searched me and you know me.
You know when I sit and when I rise; you perceive
my thoughts from afar. You discern my going out
and my lying down; you are familiar with all my ways.
Before a word is on my tongue you know it completely,
O Lord. You hem me in—behind and before;
you have laid your hand upon me. Such knowledge
is too wonderful for me, too lofty for me to attain.

Where can I go from your Spirit? Where can I flee from
your presence? If I go up to the heavens, you are there;
if I make my bed in the depths, you are there. If I rise
on the wings of the dawn, if I settle on the far
side of the sea, even there your hand will guide me,
your right hand will hold me fast. If I say, "Surely the
darkness will hide me and the light become night
around me," even the darkness will not be dark
to you; the night will shine like the day,
for darkness is as light to you....

How precious to me are your thoughts, O God!
How vast is the sum of them! Were I to count them,
they would outnumber the grains of sand.

PSALM 139:1-12, 17-19 NIV

A Prayer for Strength

O Lord, thank You for being my strength when I am weak. When I feel sad
and lonely and I call on Your name, You come and fill me with Your love.
Your promise to never leave my side helps keep me near You. Amen.

MARILYN JANSEN

Prayer Requests

Answers to Prayer

He said to me, "My grace is sufficient for you, for my power is made perfect
in weakness." Therefore I will boast all the more gladly of my weaknesses,
so that the power of Christ may rest upon me.

2 CORINTHIANS 12:9 ESV

God Be in My Heart

God be in my head, and in my understanding;
God be in my eyes, and in my looking;
God be in my mouth, and in my speaking;
God be in my heart, and in my thinking;
God be at my mine end, and at my departing.

BILLY GRAHAM

Prayer Requests

....
....
....
....
....
....
....
....

Answers to Prayer

....
....
....
....
....
....
....
....
....
....

*H*ear my voice when I call, O Lord; be merciful to me and answer me.
My heart says of you, "Seek his face!" Your face, Lord, I will seek.

PSALM 27:7-8 NIV

The Sunshine of God's Love

A joyful heart is like a sunshine of God's love, the hope of eternal happiness,
a burning flame of God.... And if we pray, we will become that sunshine of God's love—
in our own home, the place where we live, and in the world at large.

MOTHER TERESA

Prayer Requests

Answers to Prayer

Reflections and Praise

*B*ecause of the tender mercy of our God…the Sunrise from on high will visit us,
to shine upon those who sit in darkness…to guide our feet into the way of peace.

LUKE 1:78-79 NASB

Deliver Us from Evil...

Oh God, by whom we are guided in judgment,
and who raises up for us light in the darkness:
Grant us, in all our doubts and uncertainties,
that Your spirit of wisdom may save us from all false choices,
through Jesus Christ our Lord. Amen.

BOOK OF COMMON PRAYER

Prayer Requests

Answers to Prayer

The Lord will keep you from all evil; he will keep your life.
The Lord will keep your going out and your coming in
from this time forth and forevermore.

PSALM 121:7-8 ESV

My Life Is God's Prayer

If we knew how to listen, we would hear Him speaking to us.
For God does speak.... If we knew how to listen to God, if we knew
how to look around us, our whole life would become prayer.

MICHAEL QUOIST

Prayer Requests

Answers to Prayer

Reflections and Praise

$\mathcal{T}$hen GOD promises to love me all day, sing songs all through the night!
My life is God's prayer.

PSALM 42:8 THE MESSAGE

All My Cares

Thank You, God, for knowing me so well. When my little problems seem too
tiny to bring to You, remind me that You care about every aspect of my life. When the little
things grow and become really big problems, remind me that I can cast all my cares on You—
the little ones and the big ones. Amen.

MARILYN JANSEN

Prayer Requests

Answers to Prayer

Reflections and Praise

*H*umble yourselves under the mighty hand of God, that He may exalt you
in due time, casting all your care upon Him, for He cares for you.

1 PETER 5:6-7 NKJV

Faithful in Prayer

Like art, like music, like so many other disciplines, prayer can only be
appreciated when you actually spend time in it. Spending time with the
Master will elevate your thinking. The more you pray, the more will be revealed.
You will appreciate not only the greatness of prayer, but the greatness of God.

JONI EARECKSON TADA

Prayer Requests

Answers to Prayer

Be joyful in hope, patient in affliction, faithful in prayer.

ROMANS 12:12 NIV

We make mistakes, we sin, we fall down, but each time we get up and begin again. We pray again. We seek to follow God again.... We confess and begin again...and again...and again.

RICHARD J. FOSTER

Prayer of Confession

Have mercy on me, O God, because of your
unfailing love. Because of your great compassion,
blot out the stain of my sins. Wash me clean
from my guilt. Purify me from my sin.
For I recognize my rebellion; it haunts me
day and night. Against you, and you alone,
have I sinned; I have done what is evil in
your sight. You will be proved right in what
you say, and your judgment against me is just....

Purify me from my sins, and I will be clean;
wash me, and I will be whiter than snow. Oh, give
me back my joy again; you have broken me—
now let me rejoice. Don't keep looking
at my sins. Remove the stain of my guilt.

Create in me a clean heart, O God. Renew a loyal
spirit within me. Do not banish me from your
presence, and don't take your Holy Spirit from me.

Restore to me the joy of your salvation.

PSALM 51:1-4, 7-12 NLT

A Heart of Wisdom

In prayer Jesus slows us down, teaches us to count how few days we have,
and gifts us with wisdom. He reveals to us that we are so caught up
in what is urgent that we have overlooked what is essential.

BRENNAN MANNING

Prayer Requests

Answers to Prayer

Reflections and Praise

*T*each us to number our days aright, that we may gain a heart of wisdom.

PSALM 90:12 NIV

To the God Who Is There

The best reason to pray is that God is really there. In praying, our unbelief gradually
starts to melt. God moves smack into the middle of even an ordinary day....
Prayer is a matter of keeping at it.... Thunderclaps and lightning flashes are
very unlikely. It is well to start small and quietly.

EMILY GRIFFIN

Prayer Requests

Answers to Prayer

Reflections and Praise

*E*verything GOD does is right—the trademark on all his works is love.
GOD's there, listening for all who pray, for all who pray and mean it.

PSALM 145:17-18 THE MESSAGE

A Prayer for Protection

Dear Heavenly Father, please go with each member of my family each day. Protect us as we go our separate ways. Watch over each soul. When we meet again, together we will praise and worship You and give thanks for Your guidance and protection. Amen.

MARILYN JANSEN

Prayer Requests

Answers to Prayer

Reflections and Praise

May the LORD watch between you and me when we are absent one from another.

GENESIS 31:49 NKJV

For Thine Is the Kingdom and the Power...

Praise His name! He is holy. He is almighty. He is love. He brings hope,
forgiveness, heart cleansing, peace, and power. He is our deliverer
and coming King. Praise His wonderful name!

LUCILLE M. LAW

Prayer Requests

Answers to Prayer

Search high and low, scan skies and land, you'll find nothing and no one quite like GOD. The holy angels are in awe before him; he looms immense and august over everyone around him. GOD of the Angel Armies, who is like you, powerful and faithful from every angle?

PSALM 89:6-8 THE MESSAGE

A Prayer for God's Light

Dear Lord...
Shine through me, and be so in me that every soul I come in contact
with may feel Your presence in my soul.... Let me thus praise You
in the way You love best, by shining on those around me.

JOHN HENRY NEWMAN

Prayer Requests

Answers to Prayer

For it is you who light my lamp; the LORD my God lightens my darkness.

PSALM 18:28 ESV

A Prayer of Gratitude

Heavenly Father,
Thank You for loving me. I'm humbled to think that You loved me before I was
conceived in my mother's womb, and You continue to love me today. May I always
be thankful for Your love, and may I show it to those whom You have given me to love.
Always remind me of the privilege of loving and being loved in return. Amen.

KIM BOYCE

Prayer Requests

Answers to Prayer

Reflections and Praise

*F*or you created my inmost being; you knit me together in my mother's womb.
I praise you because I am fearfully and wonderfully made.

PSALM 139:13-14 NIV

Great Is the Lord

Bless You, O Lord, for the living arc of the sky over me this morning.
Bless You, O Lord, for the companionship of night mist far above the
skyscraper peaks I saw when I woke once during the night.
Bless You, O Lord, for the miracle of light to my eyes
and the mystery of it ever changing.

CARL SANDBURG

Prayer Requests

Answers to Prayer

*G*reat is the LORD, and greatly to be praised....
The LORD made the heavens.
Splendor and majesty are before him;
strength and beauty are in his sanctuary.

PSALM 96:4-6 ESV

You will go out with joy and be led forth with peace;
the mountains and the hills will break forth into shouts of joy before you,
and all the trees of the field will clap their hands.

ISAIAH 55:12 NASB

A Prayer for Peace

Lord, Make me an instrument of Thy peace.
Where there is hatred, let me sow love;
Where there is injury, pardon;
Where there is doubt, faith;
where there is despair, hope;
Where there is darkness, light;
Where there is sadness, joy.

Grant that I may not so much seek
to be consoled as to console,
to be understood as to understand,
to be loved as to love.

For it is in giving that we receive,
It is in pardoning that we are pardoned,
And it is in dying that we are born to eternal life.

FRANCIS OF ASSISI

A Time for Prayer

Where does the time go, Lord? I can't seem to get everything done in one day. Maybe I am
trying to do too many things. No matter how busy it gets, Jesus, help me to spend time with
You every single day. If I don't, slow me down so I can. Thank You, Lord. Amen.

MARILYN JANSEN

Prayer Requests

Answers to Prayer

He has made everything beautiful in its time.
He has also set eternity in the hearts of men.

ECCLESIASTES 3:11 NIV

A Prayer to the Good Shepherd

My Good Shepherd, You who have shown Your very gentle mercy to us,
...give grace and strength to me, Your little lamb, that in no tribulation
or anguish or pain may I turn away from You.

FRANCIS OF ASSISI

Prayer Requests

Answers to Prayer

The LORD is my shepherd; I shall not want.
He makes me lie down in green pastures.
He leads me beside still waters.

PSALM 23:1-2 ESV

Listening Prayer

Retire from the world each day to some private spot.... Stay in the secret
place till the surrounding noises begin to fade out of your heart and a sense
of God's presence envelops you.... Listen for the inward Voice till you learn
to recognize it.... Learn to pray inwardly every moment.

A. W. TOZER

Prayer Requests

Answers to Prayer

*B*ut when you pray, go away by yourself, shut the door behind you, and pray to
your Father in private. Then your Father, who sees everything, will reward you.

MATTHEW 6:6 NLT

Thine Is the Glory Forever....

Glorious Father, does not all nature around me praise You?... Does not the thunder praise
You as it rolls like drums in the march of the God of armies? Do not the mountains praise
You when the woods upon their summits wave in adoration? Does not the lightning write
Your name in letters of fire? Has not the whole earth a voice? And shall I, can I, silent be?

C. H. SPURGEON, ADAPTED

Prayer Requests

Answers to Prayer

*P*raise be to the LORD God…who alone does marvelous deeds.
Praise be to his glorious name forever;
may the whole earth be filled with his glory. Amen and Amen.

PSALM 73:18-19 NIV

Dearest God, help me to pray more. I forget sometimes to ask You first before I do things or make decisions. I want to share my life with You more. I need Your wisdom. I need to hear Your voice. Please help me. Amen.

MARILYN JANSEN

Prayer Requests

Answers to Prayer

Reflections and Praise

*D*evote yourselves to prayer, being watchful and thankful.

COLOSSIANS 4:2 NIV

O Lord my God, thank You for bringing this day to a close;
Thank You for giving me rest in body and soul.
Your hand has been over me and has guarded and preserved me.

DIETRICH BONHOEFFER

Prayer Requests

Answers to Prayer

The LORD bless you and keep you;
The LORD make His face shine upon you,
And be gracious to you;
The LORD lift up His countenance upon you,
And give you peace.

NUMBERS 6:24–26 NKJV

Bring us, O Lord God…to enter into that gate and dwell in that house, where there shall be no darkness nor dazzling, but one equal light; no noise nor silence, but one equal music…no ends nor beginnings, but one equal eternity; in the habitation of Your majesty and Your glory, world without end.

JOHN DONNE

Prayer Requests

Answers to Prayer

𝒯he sun shall be no more your light by day,
nor for brightness shall the moon give you light;
but the LORD will be your everlasting light,
and your God will be your glory.

ISAIAH 60:19 ESV

Walk softly.
Speak tenderly.
Pray fervently.